Shipton, Alyn
Exploring music:singing

DEMCO

EXPLORING MUSIC

Singing

Alyn Shipton

RSVP

RAINTREE
STECK-VAUGHN
P U B L I S H E R S
The Steck-Vaughn Company

Austin, Texas

Titles in the Series
Brass
Keyboards and Electronic Music
Percussion
Singing
Strings
Woodwinds

Edited by Pauline Tait
Picture research by Diana Morris
Designed by Julian Holland
Illustrator: Terry Hadler
Electronic Production: Scott Melcer

Picture acknowledgments

Raintree Steck-Vaughn Publishers would like to thank the Millfield Junior School music department, especially Mr. Brian Armfield, for assistance with commissioned photography; and David Titchener for supplying the photographs.

The author and publishers wish to thank the following photographic sources: AP/Wide World: p7 (top); Barnaby's Picture Library; p11 (top right), p15, p17 (top); BBC Photos: p28 (bottom; E.T. Archives: p8 (top); © Claude Gassian/LGI: p16; Sonia Halliday Photographs: p8 (bottom); Robert Harding Picture Library: p13, p24 (top); Image Bank: p21 (top); Kobal: p14 (bottom); Performing Arts Library: front cover, p5, p7 (top), p12, p14 (top), p24 (bottom); Redferns: p7 (bottom), p10, p16, p18 (bottom), p19, p20, p25; © Armando Gallo/Retna: p. 28 (top); Chris Walter/Relay: p29; Sam Wix/Retna p21 (bottom); © Superstock: p19; Zefa: title page, p11 (top left), p22, p26, p27 (top & bottom).

Cover credits
(Gloria Estefan) © Susan Watts/Retna; (choir) © Redferns;
(opera) © Winnie Klotz.

Library of Congress Cataloging-in-Publication Data

Shipton, Alyn.
     Singing / Alyn Shipton.
       p.   cm. — (Exploring music)
     Includes index.
     Summary: Examines vocal music throughout history, discussing how the voice works, different kinds of singing and songs, and the technology involved in recording and playing back vocal music.
     ISBN 0-8114-2315-8
     1. Singing — History — Juvenile literature.   2. Vocal music — History and criticism — Juvenile literature.   3. Sound — Recording and reproducing — Juvenile literature.   [1. Vocal music — History.   2. Singing — History. 3. Sound — Recording and reproducing.]   I. Title.   II. Series: Shipton, Alyn. Exploring music.
ML3928.S55   1994
782—dc20   93-20006
                                           CIP

73/49

Printed and bound in the United States
1 2 3 4 5 6 7 8 9 0 VHP 99 98 97 96 95 94 93

Contents

How the Voice Works

Sound

When anything vibrates, it makes a sound. When vibrations pass through the air to our ears, we hear the sound. This is because vibrations push or pull the air nearby, making sound waves that travel through the air. Different kinds of vibrations make different kinds of waves: Small vibrations make little rippling waves in the air, large throbbing vibrations make giant waves. Each type of wave makes a different sound in our ears. We can tell these sounds apart by identifying three things:

volume: how loud the sound is;

pitch: how high or low it is; and

tone: the type or quality of the sound.

NOTES AND OTHER SOUNDS

To sing a particular note, a singer learns to make the vocal cords vibrate at just the right speed and tension. He or she does this by using the throat muscles to make the vocal cords tighter or looser. Unless notes are simply hummed, a singer also has to learn to sing words, using the tongue and teeth to produce vowels and consonants. It is harder to sing some words than others because of the way the shape of the mouth has to change to make the different sounds.

The human voice has different registers, or different **ranges** of notes. Singers call the high range the **head voice,** the middle range the **throat voice,** and the lowest range the **chest voice.** To describe the very highest notes of all, especially of a tenor, singers use the Italian word **falsetto.** When men sing in the range of women's voices, they are singing falsetto notes.

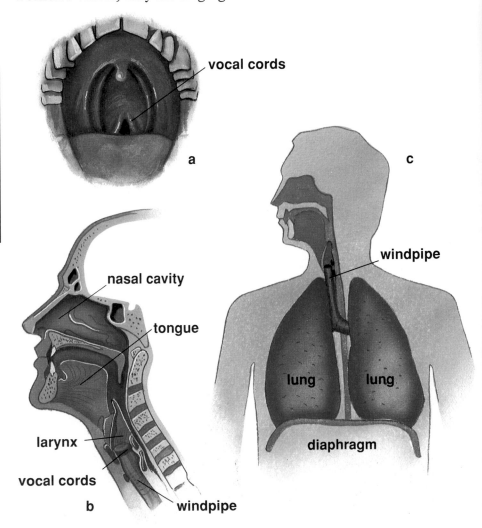

The important parts of a singer's "instrument"—the human body. Diagram (a) shows the larynx, (b) shows the head and neck, and (c) shows the lungs and diaphragm.

The Voice

Thinking of the voice as an instrument helps us to understand how it works, and how singers learn to use it.

Just like a woodwind instrument, the voice works when air is forced past the vocal cords and made to vibrate. The vocal cords are at the top of the windpipe, and they work like a **free reed**. Air from the lungs is pushed up past the vocal cords by a wall of muscle called the diaphragm. The singer, just like the instrumental player, controls volume, pitch, and tone.

volume This depends on the amount of air that is pushed past the vocal cords.

pitch This is controlled by the length of the vocal cords and how fast they vibrate. Women's voices are higher than men's, since they have shorter vocal cords.

tone The tone, or timbre, of each voice depends on each individual person. The size and shape of the mouth and throat affect tone, just as the size and shape of an instrument do.

When singers are trained, they learn how to control the shape of their mouths to produce the best tone. They also learn how to breathe correctly to get the best volume of sound. In addition, they learn to care for their voices, to keep them healthy and working properly.

This picture shows the opera singer Dame Kiri Te Kanawa and how she controls the shape of her mouth and throat to project the best sound.

People's Voices

Everybody's voice is unique. No two men and no two women sound exactly alike. Women's, girls', men's, and boys' voices can be grouped into similar types according to the range of notes that they can sing. Some women have very high voices, called **soprano** voices; some men have very deep voices called **bass** voices. The full range of voices, from the top downward, is as follows: soprano; mezzo-soprano; alto, contralto or countertenor; tenor; baritone; bass.

The illustrations show the range of each type of voice.

This is how people's voices are grouped by range:
Girls: soprano, alto
Women: soprano, mezzo-soprano, and contralto
Boys: soprano, alto
Men: alto or countertenor, tenor, baritone, and bass

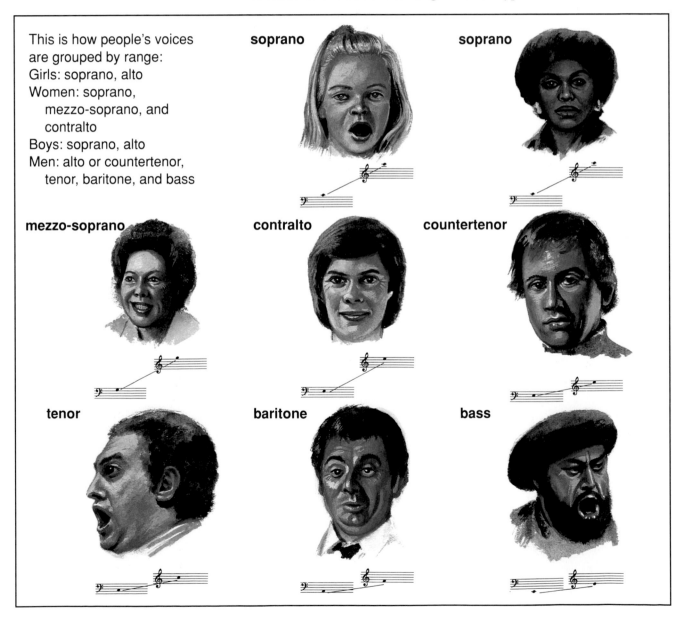

BOYS' AND GIRLS' VOICES

Throughout history, composers have written for the sound of soprano voices, singing alone or in choirs. Today, many cathedral and church choirs include girls and boys, but until the mid-20th century only boys' voices sang the highest parts. Musicians valued the clear, pure sound that the best boy sopranos have starting at about the age of seven. Later (between the ages of 11 and 14) boys' vocal cords grow to a size that forces their voices to drop in pitch, and their voices "*break*." Girls' voices do not go through the same sudden change, though most women's voices deepen as they get older.

A small number of boy sopranos have such outstanding voices that they become famous during the few years before their voices change. Aled Jones made many outstanding recordings of music for treble voice, like the opening of the carol "Once In Royal David's City," or the **anthem** "O For the Wings of a Dove."

In many parts of the world, boys' choirs have been formed. Some, like the Boys Choir of Harlem, travel all over the world to sing. Some composers have used these choirs as a special feature in their music, like Britten's *Spring Symphony*, in which the boys' voices imitate the sound of children playing. Such highly trained choirs (particularly in cathedrals) often go to special schools, and as well as the normal subjects, there are extra lessons in both singing and voice.

The life of a chorister can be hard, learning new music every day, practicing for concerts, broadcasts, and recordings, as well as normal school work and sports!

Members of the Boys Choir of Harlem come from all over New York City, with many from Central Harlem. This group gives special emphasis to works by African-American composers, to spirituals, and to early American music.

Aled Jones

7

Singing Together

A troubadour entertains a courtly lady in this 15th-century manuscript painting. He is singing to his own lute accompaniment.

The earliest songs were long stories set to music, sung by one person to an audience. These songs were about great and heroic events. We also know that people sang together as they worked or traveled, as they still do. They also sing to relax, to celebrate when work is over, or as part of a religion.

People have made up songs about all kinds of subjects. Love songs, sung to a lute or guitar accompaniment, date from the 12th century and were sung by traveling singers called **troubadours**. Other early singers were called **jongleurs**. They performed plays and acrobatic shows as well, traveling through Europe and North Africa.

A 9th-century manuscript shows Pope Gregory dictating chants.

CHANTS AND PLAINSONG

Almost no music for singers was written down until about 400 years ago, except in the Christian church. So we cannot be certain about what types of singing besides religious singing were then common. Chanting **psalms** has been part of Jewish music since the destruction of the Temple in Jerusalem by the Romans in A.D. 70, when instrumental music was banned, and people sang instead. A **chant** is a short musical phrase repeated over and over again.

From the 4th century onward, Christians sang a kind of chant called **plainsong**. Everyone sang the same melody (singing in **unison**). A book of these chants was collected in the time of Pope Gregory at the end of the 6th century. The style became known as Gregorian chanting. Two common types of chants split the choir into two, singing questions and answer phrases.

PART SINGING

In plainsong, everybody sings the same note. Over 1,000 years ago, choirs started to sing in a more interesting way. To start with, one group of people sang the melody, while another group sang the same melody five notes higher. This style is called *organum*.

By the start of the 11th century, choirs had several parts or voices that were independent of one another. One type of song they sang was the **round,** or **canon.** One group sings the melody, then a second starts the tune again when the first group completes the first line. As the next group finishes the line, another joins in and so on. The famous early English **part-song** "Sumer is icumen in" dates from 1250.

As more and more parts were written for different voices singing at the same time, the style began to be called **polyphony** (which means "many sounds"). In the church, part-songs for many voices were called **motets.** Witty and entertaining part-songs called **madrigals** were also sung for entertainment and enjoyment away from the church. In 1601, a group of 21 English composers wrote a collection of madrigals praising Queen Elizabeth I called *The Triumphs of Oriana*.

Choral Singing

If you want to sing in a choir, there are many opportunities. For girls and boys few things are more exhilarating than singing with a large group of other people in one of the great choral pieces. Some areas offer youth choirs, many schools have choirs, and there are usually chances to audition. You will learn to read music, how to breathe as you sing, and how to sing in tune with everyone else! You will practice together and learn about working as a team to get the most satisfying results.

The manuscript of "Sumer is icumen in." The black letters give the words in medieval English, and below them the red letters give a Latin translation.

Motets, Cantatas, and Oratorios

Motets were written between about 1250 and 1750. They usually had between four and six voices (or parts) and were usually sung unaccompanied. The great composers in this style included Josquin Desprez, Lassus, and Palestrina.

In Germany and Austria, composers in the 1700s wrote **cantatas** and **oratorios**. An oratorio is a piece written for choir, orchestra, and solo singers that tells a story—usually from the Bible. Cantatas are shorter pieces, usually about a single incident. Michael Haydn, for example, wrote a Christmas cantata about the shepherds who came to Christ's birth. It lasts about ten minutes. Handel's oratorio *Messiah*, in contrast, tells much of the story of Jesus' life and lasts over two hours.

By the 1800s and 1900s, composers were using choirs to sing in big orchestral compositions, like the symphonies of Beethoven, Mahler, and Britten. Some of the world's finest choirs are those that sing with particular symphony orchestras.

OTHER PART-SONGS

In Wales, there are male-voice choirs that sing hymns and traditional Welsh songs. In the United States a small-scale version of this style is the barbershop quartet, or the gospel quartets of the southern states. In England, starting in the 1600s, people sang glees, boisterous songs about food, drink, hunting, and love. These were sung by glee clubs and other amateur groups. Other kinds of choirs sing the traditional songs of South Africa, with European part-singing adapted to local rhythms and harmonies.

The Kennedy High School Gospel Choir, singing at the New Orleans Heritage Festival, demonstrates the energetic style of gospel singing heard in many churches in the area.

A symphony chorus made up of several choirs singing with a full orchestra, like this one in New Zealand, is a thrilling sound.

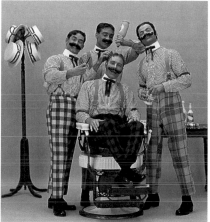

Barbershop quartet members often wear fancy outfits to perform their witty songs.

Listening Guide

There are many types of recorded choral music: short pieces, long pieces, funny pieces, and serious pieces. The shortest include pieces written by the American composer William Billings, some of whose tunes, like "Jargon," last less than a minute. Youth groups sing pieces like "Jonah Man Jazz" or "The Daniel Jazz."

Modern pieces like John Gardner's "Proverbs of Hell" often have special effects written into them. Others like Toch's famous "Geographical Fugue" have musical jokes. In Toch's fugue, the names of the places are spoken, not sung. Plainsong and motets by Josquin, Palestrina, Lassus, and Praetorius have been recorded by many early music groups. Cantatas by Schutz, Telemann, and Vivaldi have been recorded by cathedral and college choirs. The big oratorios of Bach and Handel have been recorded by symphony orchestras and choruses like those of London, New York, and St. Louis. Symphonies and oratorios that include choirs are Mahler's 8th, Beethoven's 9th, Britten's *Spring Symphony*, and Walton's *Belshazzar's Feast*. Gospel choirs have made many recordings like those by the Mormon Tabernacle Choir or the London Community Gospel Choir.

Opera

An opera is a play with music, in which the main characters sing, rather than speak, their parts. Most operas are performed on stage, just like a play, and this is what makes them different from oratorios, where the music is performed in a concert with no **set** and staging.

One of the first operas was Monteverdi's *Orfeo*—the story of Orpheus. This was first performed in 1607, in Mantua, Italy. Soon, opera caught on, and theaters called "opera houses" were specially built to present this mixture of music and drama. Early productions had complex stage machinery that made special effects like waves and clouds. By the late 19th century, singers had become the most important part of opera, but even today some operas are still given special productions, with dramatic effects. Sometimes real horses and other animals are used on stage in the crowd scenes.

WHO MAKES AN OPERA?

Operas are the most complicated form of drama, and many people work together to make them successful. The opera is written by a **composer** (who creates the music) and a **librettist** (who writes the words that are sung and spoken).

Operas often have very colorful sets and costumes, like this scene from Bizet's opera *Carmen*.

The **producer** takes charge of directing the singers and actors on stage. The **conductor** directs the music from the orchestra pit (a space between the audience and the stage where the orchestra plays, set below ground level).

On stage, the main roles, which usually have the most difficult and demanding music, are sung by soloists. Long solo songs are called arias. Most operas also have a chorus—a choir of men and women who act and sing all the supporting roles. They may be asked to be anything from pirates to townspeople or factory workers. The singers are rehearsed by a **vocal coach,** who helps them learn the music and words. The coach is nearby during the performance, either below the front of the stage or beside it (in the **wings**). If singers momentarily forget their parts, the prompter will help them. In many theaters the coach gives signals about when to start and stop to singers who are out of sight of the conductor.

A vocal coach teaches two singers their roles in an opera.

Listening Guide

Britten's *Let's Make an Opera* was written to introduce children to opera. Children and parents take major parts. Gian Carlo Menotti wrote his children's opera *Amahl and the Night Visitors* for television. Other operas written for TV include Britten's *Owen Wingrave*. There are many opera films including Bizet's *Carmen* and Verdi's great operas like *Aida* and *La Traviata*.

This view of an opera on stage, seen from across the orchestra pit, shows how singers and instrumentalists follow the directions of the conductor.

Musicals

In Andrew Lloyd Webber's *Phantom of the Opera*, actor and singer Michael Crawford is concealed behind the hero's elaborate mask.

The musical is the most popular kind of stage play with music. The first musicals grew out of light and comic operas in the early 20th century. The best of them have many well-known songs. One of the hallmarks of a musical came to be a lavish production with complex sets and stage machinery. Few of the great musicals can be put on by school or amateur groups without large and well-equipped stages.

Jerome Kern's *Showboat* is set on the steamboats of the Mississippi River. Cole Porter's *Kiss Me Kate* is based on Shakespeare's *Taming of the Shrew*. Romantic subjects like this are common in musicals, and many of them have been made into films. Some of the best musical films to watch are Lerner and Loewe's *My Fair Lady* and *Camelot*, Rodgers and Hammerstein's *Oklahoma!*, *South Pacific*, and *The Sound of Music*. Most dramatic of all musical films is Leonard Bernstein's *West Side Story*, a modern version of Shakespeare's *Romeo and Juliet*, set in the tougher neighborhoods of New York.

The songs from many musicals appeared first on records and tapes. This made them famous before the musical itself was performed in the theater. Many shows by Andrew Lloyd Webber, including *Joseph and the Technicolor Dreamcoat*, *Jesus Christ Superstar*, and *Evita* started out on records. There are recordings of Lloyd Webber's other shows, most of which have stunning special effects, like *Starlight Express*, *The Phantom of the Opera*, and *Cats*.

In this scene from *West Side Story* rival New York gangs, the Jets and the Sharks, fight.

Some musicals are so popular that they are performed in the theater for years. Many such shows are put on in theaters all around the world. *Les Misérables*, by Claude-Michel Schönberg, is one play that has been performed in many cities. Other shows that were famous in the past are rediscovered and put on again, including *Me and My Gal* (originally written in 1937) and *The Boy Friend* (from 1953).

Dorothy Gale meets the tin man, the cowardly lion, and the scarecrow in the musical version of *Wizard of Oz*, which has songs by Harold Arlen.

MUSIC IN FILMS

In the theater, most musicals have several songs, or "numbers," and between them the play is acted and spoken. For a film production, there is usually music all the way through. Even if the actors are speaking, there will be background music just as in any TV program or film based on a play. This means the composer has to write more music, or sometimes another composer is asked to write the extra material. The film actors lip-synch to a recorded version of the songs. Sometimes, they even lip-synch to other people's voices. When the film has been shot, and is **edited**, the soundtrack is often recorded again to make sure the highest quality music fits the finished film exactly.

Songs of Many Kinds

Church music, choral music, and musical theater pieces are all written down. Many of the songs sung throughout history, however, have been passed on from singer to singer and never written down at all. Early in the 20th century, song collectors traveled throughout the world searching out these songs. They jotted them down or recorded them, after portable sound recording machines had been invented.

WORK SONGS

All kinds of jobs seem easier if you can sing while you're working. Sailors used to sing sea chanteys in the days of sailing ships as they hauled up the sails or wound in the anchor, to keep a team of men moving together in rhythm. Out in the cotton fields of the south, workers sang as they worked. The folksinger Leadbelly made records of songs like "Pick a Bale of Cotton." As the construction gangs built the canals and roads of the 1700s and 1800s, they sang songs. Some of these had question and answer phrases, but all of them helped to keep picks and shovels swinging together in the rhythm of the song. Even convicts, who were condemned to do hard labor, sang songs. Bob Marley's "Working in a Chain Gang" commemorates the words and music of prisoners.

Bob Marley

FOLK SONGS

People from many countries have songs that have been handed down from father to son and from mother to daughter. Some of these songs are solos, sung by one person around the fire in the evening, or lullabies sung to a child. Others, like the songs of the Native Americans or the Maoris of New Zealand, are sung by whole groups of people, from villages to entire tribes. Some songs are used to encourage rain to fall, or to celebrate a successful harvest. The Maori *waiata* is sung when somebody dies, after a village has gathered for the funeral.

Many **folk songs** go with traditional dances. Gypsy people, who travel all over Europe and North Africa, have many songs in their Romany language. Composers like Béla Bartók and Ralph Vaughan Williams collected songs like these. Because of the work they did, we understand more about the music that people sang as they went about their daily lives many years ago. Both of these composers used the melodies they had collected in their own music, and folk songs appear in their symphonies and chamber music.

In the United States, many songs arrived with the settlers who came from other parts of the world. Dvořák used some of these melodies from folk songs and spirituals in his symphony *From the New World*. Aaron Copland put these melodies in his music for the ballets *Billy the Kid* and *Rodeo*.

Maoris singing and performing the traditional *poi* dance.

Bartók used a cylinder recorder to capture the sounds of Hungarian folksongs in the early years of the 20th century.

17

Blues and Jazz Singing

Bessie Smith

Many kinds of songs were sung by the black population in the southern United States. The workers in the cotton fields around the Mississippi River, and on the docksides of southern ports like New Orleans, developed their own music. Their singing included the rhythms of African music, as many black American families had originally come to the United States as slaves from Africa. There were many religious songs that have survived today as gospel songs and spirituals, like "Deep River," "Go Down Moses," and "Swing Low, Sweet Chariot." Out in the countryside of the Mississippi delta, a new style began around 1900, as people sang songs of deep sadness that became known as the blues.

BLUES SINGING

Most blues songs are poems with many verses. Each verse has three lines, the first two the same, like:

Don't the moon look lonesome shining through them trees,
Don't the moon look lonesome shining through them trees,
Don't your house look lonesome when your baby packs to leave.

Robert Cray is a young blues singer who has kept the blues tradition alive.

Louis Armstrong demonstrating his jazz style of "scat" singing.

By the 1920s, blues records were being made. The best of these sad songs have catchy tunes that people quickly learned to hum or whistle. They could be heard by people all over America, and around the world, on records. Some of the most famous blues singers were the women who became known as the "classic" blues singers of the 1920s: Bessie Smith, Mamie Smith, Ma Rainey, and Sara Martin.

Bessie Smith was the most famous of them all and was called the "empress of the blues." She made many records and toured the theaters and vaudeville shows of the United States.

When the blues singers of the country moved to the cities of the northern United States to find work, their music became harder and they **amplified** their guitars. The new style was called rhythm and blues, and it was sung by people like Muddy Waters and B.B. King.

JAZZ SINGING

Jazz music flowered at the same time as the blues, and many blues singers sang on jazz records. The best jazz singers learned to **improvise,** in other words, to compose as they went along, singing new melodies to nonsense words. This style was called "scat" singing. It was started by Louis Armstrong when he dropped the piece of paper with the words to a song during a recording session. He continued singing, making up silly words of his own, so as not to spoil the recording.

Singers like Ella Fitzgerald and Sarah Vaughan sang jazz songs and could also sing "scat" solos. Billie Holiday was another great jazz singer, and though her life is a tragic story of drug addiction, she could make audiences cry with her beautiful singing. Her song "Strange Fruit" was an early song of protest for black Americans' civil rights.

Singing Through a Sound System

If you go to a giant rock concert at an outdoor arena, or in a vast theater, you'll see singers using amplification. There are microphones to pick up the sound of the voices and complicated equipment to make the sounds loud enough to be heard by the entire audience.

THE MICROPHONE

Early microphones almost obscured the face of the singer. They were hung on heavy stands that were difficult to move, and the singer had to sing closely into the microphone. Wires ran from the microphone to the **amplifier**.

A microphone turns sounds into electric signals. An amplifier strengthens the electric signals and loudspeakers convert these stronger signals back into sound. Modern technology has altered some of the ways in which this happens. Today's microphones (or "mikes") are radio mikes, with no cables, just a short stubby aerial that sends the signal back to the amplifier. This allows a singer to move freely on stage without falling over microphone wires. Most microphones are hand-held, but for singers who want to keep both hands free, for example in a musical play, body mikes are used. These send their signals back from a little transmitter the size of a pack of cards.

George Michael uses a radio mike.

THE AMPLIFIER

Amplifiers used to have rows of wires snaking into them from microphones. Now there is a receiver unit that decodes the signals from radio microphones. Amplifiers used in today's rock concerts are very powerful, and they are usually operated by a **sound engineer** from a **mixing console**. They all work in the same way, by allowing the operator to control the "gain." Gain is the strength of the signal passed on to the speakers.

The sound engineer's view of a mixing console, looking through the studio glass to the pianist being recorded.

LOUDSPEAKERS

At the back of every loudspeaker is a powerful magnet. The electric signals from the amplifier make the magnet push or pull the **cone** of the speaker. This pushes or pulls the air around it and recreates the sound originally picked up by the microphone.

The loudspeakers at rock concerts are very large versions of the ones found in most radios and cassette players. They are arranged in huge "stacks" to project the sound of the music to the whole audience. The sound from a stack goes away from the performers on the stage, so they cannot hear themselves as the audience does. But small monitor or "foldback" speakers are placed in front of musicians so they can hear themselves.

The Live Aid concert in London and Philadelphia in 1985 was one of the biggest-ever outdoor concerts, held to raise money to feed starving people in Africa. Giant screens showed close-ups of the performers in London, and there were huge stacks of speakers to relay the sound.

The Mixing Console

A close-up of the mixing console shows how each microphone is controlled by a sliding switch called a "fader."

When a concert or a show is amplified, the sound engineer controls what the audience actually hears. The signal from each microphone passes through the mixing console on its way to the amplifier.

A mixing console has rows of controls—one for each microphone. The sound engineer **balances** the volume between the various microphones. This allows every musician to be properly heard and mixes the results into one "output signal."

The sound engineer and the mixing console are usually placed out in the audience of a concert and not on the stage with the performers. This allows the engineer to set the volume at the right level for the audience. Some sound engineers use headphones or "cans" to listen to the signal from each microphone and adjust it correctly, but they have to rely on their ears alone to get the level right for an audience.

From a console placed in the audience area, an engineer controls sound level.

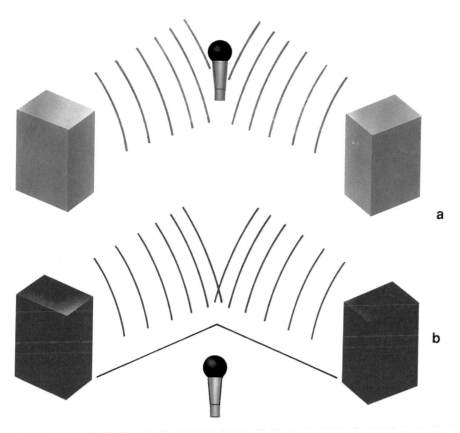

Feedback occurs when the microphone picks up sound waves from the loudspeakers (a). Feedback can be prevented by moving the mike to a position where the waves move past it (b).

a

b

FEEDBACK

Sometimes rock concerts are interrupted by a terrible howling noise from the loudspeakers. This is called "feedback," and it happens when the microphone picks up the sounds of the loudspeakers and amplifies them again. This is why speaker stacks are usually placed in front of or beside stages with singers and microphones, so that the microphones cannot pick up the sounds from the speakers.

EFFECTS

Instrumentalists like guitarists and keyboard players can often change the sounds of their instruments by using "effects boxes" that add echoes and other changes to their sound. Singers have to rely on the sound engineer for most effects. Among the controls on the mixing console are switches that can add echoes or "reverb" (short for reverberation). A good sound engineer uses the console to give a singer the best tone and depth when the voice is amplified. The sound engineer also decides on the "spread" of sound. This is the place that each sound seems to be coming from.

Stereo sound has different sounds coming from each speaker. The engineer decides which stereo "channel" (left or right) will be occupied by a microphone. The engineer can also "balance" the sound between speakers, by having part of the sound from a microphone coming out of one speaker and part through the other. Finally, the engineer can "filter" out certain sounds. This is easy to do with an automated mixing console, which uses a computer to control the sounds. The computer can eliminate some **frequencies** altogether.

The Recording Studio

In the control room of a recording studio, the operator works from a sheet of notes that tell her how to adjust the console as the performance progresses.

There are two parts to most recording or broadcasting studios. The first part, called the control room, contains a mixing console very similar to that used by the sound engineer at a concert. It also houses the recording equipment, which consists of either ordinary tape recorders or digital tape machines. The second part is the studio itself, where the performance takes place.

Some studios are very large and can house a whole symphony orchestra. The BMG studios in New York are like this. Others are smaller and more suitable for recording chamber music or solo performers. Usually, the cubicle and the studio are separated by a thick, soundproof glass screen.

IN THE STUDIO

Most studios are designed to have a special kind of sound quality. Absorbent material reduces **reverberation** (mistakenly called "echo"), giving what recording engineers call a very "dry" sound. Studio microphones are very sensitive and can pick up tiny sounds, so the recording studio is designed to exclude outside noises. Each musician has his or her own microphone, and these are connected to the mixing console in the control room. The engineer sets a level for each microphone before recording begins, and as the music is performed, a meter shows the engineer the level of sound coming from each microphone. If the level is set too high, the meter reading will be in the red zone, and the engineer reduces the recording level to prevent distortion. Distortion introduces a nasty, unpleasant quality to the recorded sound, and it is the engineer's goal to keep it at a minimum.

Some studios are very large and can house many performers and large instruments. Other studios are small, for soloists.

MULTITRACK RECORDING

At a concert, or on a recording, all the parts of a performance are heard together. By putting the sound of each microphone onto a separate part of the tape (called a "track"), a recording can be made a piece at a time—rock music is often recorded this way. First a "click" track giving the basic beat is recorded. Then one by one the other parts are added. Each performer listens to the clicks over headphones to keep time. When all the parts are recorded, the click track is not used, leaving a finished performance that sounds as if it was all recorded together. These techniques are so accurate that different tracks can be added in other studios at a later date. Paul Simon has made albums with parts recorded on different days in different cities!

Singers often record their vocals over a prerecorded instrumental track. Listening to the group or an orchestra on headphones, they sing alone in the studio—and they can do it again if a mistake is made.

In this view of the control room and studio, the members of a big band who are being recorded can be seen in the distance. Each has a microphone linked to a different channel, or "track," on the console in the foreground. Vocalists may record their parts later, once the band tracks are finished. Some of the musicians wear headphones, or "cans," so they can clearly hear how their own part will sound.

Singing on Film and Television

When we see a singer on television or in a film, the performance may have been made in several different ways. It might be a live television performance, relayed exactly as it happens. It might be all or part of a recorded performance from a theater or concert hall. It might be a studio performance. It might even be a clever mixture of pictures with a prerecorded soundtrack, with the singer lip-synching to his or her own performance.

REMOTE BROADCASTS

A live concert, or a recording from a theater or concert hall, is often called a "remote broadcast." This means that it is recorded outside the film or TV studios, using portable sound equipment. Engineers set up microphones that will not get in the way of performers, or the audience, at the event. The recording is controlled from a mobile mixing console, usually outside the site. The cameras are set up as well, and the director coordinates sound and vision from the control van. For television, the director will have several TV screens showing the pictures from each camera, and the picture will be "cut" from one to another to fit the music. The results are recorded on videotape.

A TV production team selects the pictures from a number of cameras.

Because film cameras do not transmit pictures, it is not possible for the director to see the picture being taken by each camera when a film, rather than a video, is made. Instead, the camera operators follow instructions from the director. Sound and pictures are recorded separately, and edited together when the film is developed. The best pictures are literally cut from the film taken by each camera and stuck together in sequence.

Film editing is done by experts in an "editing suite." When the best shots have been joined, a special editing machine plays back the film at the same time as the music. Sound and pictures are **synchronized,** and a third "voice over" track can be added to sound recorded at the time. Sometimes the complete soundtrack has to be re-recorded by studio musicians who try to make their performance fit the pictures exactly.

Editing is also done from videotape. This is a TV editing suite where video images are being cut together.

STUDIO PERFORMANCES

Music filmed or taped in a studio is often of better quality than remote broadcasts. Cameras, lights, and microphones can be controlled more accurately. Many television concerts are performed in TV studios, and the tapes can then be edited afterward to show viewers the "highlights" of the performance, and to cut out many of the pauses between pieces.

Part of this concert by a folk group is recorded in a German TV studio.

Making a Rock Video

A shot from a rock video being recorded.

Most rock videos are expensive productions that are made in just the same way as the spectacular sequences of film musicals. The same crew and technical apparatus that made a film like *The Sound of Music* are needed to make most three-minute videos.

Rock videos are made after the music has been recorded (for sale on tape or compact disc), so the musicians will lip-synch to the recording. The director of the video and the singers work out a storyboard. This plans all the scenes that are going to be used and establishes where they will fit the song. Some may be shot in a studio, others may be shot on **location**. If other actors or dancers are going to be used, their scenes are planned in minute detail because these will be the most costly to shoot.

TV Rock Singing
When you watch a TV program that has groups or singers in the studio singing their current songs, usually it has been made the same way as a video. Few groups want to perform a song "live" that may have taken weeks of studio work to perfect, so they lip-synch their performances to their recordings. The studio audience has to look as if they are hearing the group perform their song, but in reality they are only hearing the recording! Some famous groups began by lip-synching to the voices of other singers altogether! Here Status Quo, a British group, makes a studio appearance on a popular TV show.

FILMING A SCENE IN A VIDEO

Some videos are filmed and edited on film before being issued
as videotapes. Others are recorded straight onto videotape. The
method is the same. A section is selected from the storyboard.
Then a set is built or a location is found. The best position for the
cameras is chosen, and the giant lights used for filming are set up.
Sometimes a short length of track is put down so a heavy camera
can be moved quickly and silently during filming. Sometimes a
camera is mounted on a crane.

Speakers are set up to play back the sound of the recording.
Then the performers arrive. They are put into position on the set,
and filming begins. At the start of each section of film, at the very
moment the section of the recording begins, a blackboard with a
clapper on it is put in front of the camera. This "clapperboard"
has details of the scene chalked on it, and the loud crack of the
clapper is used to synchronize the soundtrack and the pictures.

Some complex videos involve dozens of "extras" (actors or
dancers). Michael Jackson's 14-minute video *Thriller*, or Elton
John's *I'm Still Standing*, had long dance sequences that had to
be worked out very carefully.

Michael Jackson performs on the
set of his *Beat It* video.

Glossary

amplifier an electronic device that increases the loudness of sounds

amplify increase the loudness of a sound

anthem a setting of religious words to music, often words of praise or gladness

aria a song, sometimes part of a longer piece of music

balance making the musical sounds from different areas match each other correctly

bass the lowest adult male voice

canon a piece of music in which different singers or groups of singers follow one another, singing the same line that the group before has just sung

cantata a short oratorio (*See* oratorio)

chant a short musical phrase that is repeated over and over

chest voice the lowest singing voice

composer the person who creates a piece of music

conductor the person who controls the musicians or singers when they are performing

cone the cone-shaped part of a speaker that produces the sound

edit put voice and movement together on a film or video so that they match

falsetto the highest voice that can be used by an adult male

folk song a song, often well-known within a particular country, for which there is no known composer

free reed	a reed, usually of metal, fastened at only one end
frequency	number of vibrations that can occur within a given period of time, for example a second
head voice	the highest singing voice
improvise	make up words or music as the player or singer goes along
jongleur	a traveling minstrel in medieval times
librettist	the writer of the words in an opera or oratorio
lip-synch	silently mouthing the words of the song to match a recording of that song
location	where a film or video is made, or shot
madrigal	a part-song for several voices
mixing console	where sounds are controlled or "mixed" by the sound engineer
motet	an anthem, usually sung with no musical accompaniment
oratorio	a musical composition that often tells a story, or part of a story, often with a religious theme
part-song	a song in which the lines are sung by various voices often following each other as in a canon or a round
pitch	the level of a note, indicated by its position on the scale
plainsong	a chant sung in unison
polyphony	music in which two or more melodies are sounded at the same time in harmony
producer	in opera, the person who directs the singers and actors on the stage
prompter	reminds singers in a performance if they forget the words
psalm	sacred song, found in the Book of Psalms in the Old Testament of the Bible
range	the scope of a voice, from the lowest to the highest
resonance	sound that goes on longer because of the vibrations
round	a song, like a canon or part-song, that is sung over and over again, in the round
set	the furnishings for a stage in a musical production or play, including the backdrops and scenery
soprano	the highest female voice
sound engineer	the person who controls the sound the audience hears
synchronize	occur at the same time
throat voice	the middle range of the voice
tone	the quality or clarity of a sound
troubadour	French poet-musician of the 1100s and 1200s
unison	singing together at the same pitch
vocal coach	the person who helps singers to learn the words, especially in opera
volume	how loud a sound is
wings	the sides of the stage

Index